ALLEYCAT

MARK DONACHIE

Editing: Emma Greer
Cover design and book layout: Melvin Creative Ltd

To my younger self

Contents

Chapter One

Pain

please don't go
I will get on my knees
and beg if I need to
desperate or not
because I have already
lost enough
and I cannot
lose you too

- stay

the moment you left
I put my back to the door
and screamed so hard
the floorboards cracked
and the windows smashed

- pain

Alleycat

the messages
you never sent
that you promised you would
sent the message
loud and clear

- ironic

although I broke up with you
the only person that got broken
was me

- the hurt

Alleycat

I hate that my phone
tells me the last time
you were on yours
so that I know
when you last spoke
to someone else
but what I hate most
is that now
it never shines
as bright
as it used to

- modern sadness

every other craving I have had
seems minuscule to this
I can stop myself smoking
I can stop myself drinking
but I cannot stop myself
missing
aching
screaming
crying
over you

- bad habits

Alleycat

you asked me
to come over for the evening
I came without hesitation
but all you wanted
was intoxication
mixed with escalation
and I woke up
to the painful realisation
that you did not want me
the same way I wanted you

- different pages

when you walk into my flat
only then do the lights go on
because I feel
I can only glow
when you are here

- insecure

I cannot bear
to look in the mirror
and see the version of myself
I have become
because this is the version
the pain has made me
and I just want
to feel myself again

- man in the mirror

no longer
do I tell you my dreams
for all you do
is shoot them down

- firing line

I can battle rain
but this feels like a hurricane

- drowning in the sadness

I need you to confirm
that you left me
for someone else
so I can give my heart
something to work with

- the remedy

Alleycat

my eyelids
hugged each other
as they could not
look to witness
you walk away
for the second time

- second chance

Mark Donachie

I wish
I could fall out of love
the same way I fell in

- the hard part

Alleycat

I have videos of you
on my phone
that I cannot
bring myself to watch
because the moment your voice
touches my ears
my eyesight goes blurry

- fragile

how sad it is
for me
to intentionally walk past
your bus stop
on my way home
in the hope that
if you see me
it might suddenly
make you miss me

- struggling to let go

Alleycat

are you still with him
because part of me
is still with you
and another part
belongs to someone new

- missing pieces

I should have known
every time you ignored me
when I said
I cannot wait to see you
or every time
you would tell me
to be quiet
when I asked
about our future
that it was not because
you wanted to take it slow
it was because
you never wanted us to move

- road blocks

Alleycat

tell me why
the ones that are meant
to love me most
are the ones
that have broken my heart

- coming out

I should have known
the night of that party
where I met some of your friends
that you were
never serious about us
because when asked
how you knew me
all you could say
was that we see each other
as if we were
nothing more
than two neighbours
who regularly pass each other
in the stairwell
exchanging a friendly hello

- acquaintances

Alleycat

you told me to forget
you ever existed
but how can I forget
when your existence
is the reason for mine

- soul mate

the worst heartbreak
is the one where there is
no one to blame
except circumstance

- timing

A l l e y c a t

when it is late at night
and I am laying in bed
my heart breaks in my chest
because I know
that while I am lying there
under the covers on my own
looking at old photos of us
wishing you were here
that he is under you
looking up at the eyes
I used to call home

- insomnia

why is it
only after we have ended
that all I think about
are the good parts of what we had
like how you kissed me
in every room of your apartment
just so you had the memory
or how I bought the ingredients
for your weekly cooking class
that you were too busy to buy
because I wanted
to make you smile
it is only these
kinds of memories
that I can recall
and all the bad
seem to have vanished
just like you

- get out of my head

Alleycat

it was how you decided
to leave
then decided
you wanted to be friends
then decided
you wanted to kiss me
then finally decided
we were not meant to be

- mind games

the thing that hurts me most
is that you are not hurting at all

- foolish

a human being
should never have to feel
that they have disappointed
their family or friends
because of the person
they choose to love

- sexuality

why do I let you stay
even though I know
in the morning
you will be gone
before breakfast

- loneliness

Alleycat

how is it fair
that the first time
I choose love over fear
it ends in tears
and sets the scene
for the years to come

- the pain of choosing love

if only
you were as comfortable
with your sexuality
as you were on the nights
you spent on my couch
when you loved me for hours

- denial

if it were possible
to cry away memories
I would be in luck
because by now
I would not even
remember your name

- crying you out

is it not sad
how we were once
each other's oxygen
but now when we pass
one another in the street
we do not even
open our mouths
to say hello

- perhaps it is for the best

Alleycat

how can I
expect my body
to function at fully capacity
when all I do
is treat it so poorly

- vicious circles

all this time
I thought you adored me
but in reality
it was only temporary
until you found
someone better

- player

Alleycat

if you ever come back
I will still remember
how you like your coffee
milk and two sugars
not sweet enough
a bit like
how you treated me

- sweetener

to this day
my chest still tightens
when I pass your town

- the heart never forgets

Alleycat

I either show
no emotion
or so much at once
for this is all
I have ever known

- I am sorry

how am I supposed
to tell the butterflies
in my stomach
that you do not
care about them anymore

- they only fly for you

Alleycat

my eyes
become broken taps
that will not turn off
when I think about
how you are not here anymore
if only we knew
how much you needed us
we would have been there
it is not your fault
this world can be a terrible place
but I wish
you would have stayed
and we could have
fought it together

- grief

when I think about
being with someone else
my heart frowns
and walks away in despair
because it knows
no one will ever compare
and that you
are the only one it beats for

- frustration

how can I
be raised wrong
when all I have done
is grow into myself

- unfair expectations

no one
has ever stayed
when they promised they would
so why would you
be any different

- pessimist

Alleycat

it is not my pain
I am feeling
it is the pain
of the love you left behind
in order to be with me
which I now wish
never happened

- look what you have done

you said
you wanted us to end
so you could focus on yourself
but it has only been
a few weeks
and already you are
focusing on the camera
taking the photo
of you and your new lover

- liar

Alleycat

the place
I used to call home
is now nothing more
than a house
I used to live in

- a cat in the big city

the hospital visits
are the worst
for the pain of telling
these receptionists
how I feel on the inside
while they show me
no emotion in return
hurts every time

- suffering

Alleycat

I do not understand
how you can walk away
after so many years
as if it were nothing
how on one random Monday
you can just wake up
and decide that
our most recent conversation
is our last

- I thought you cared

as I sit
in this exam hall
my stomach is in flames
because what the doctors
promised would help me
has only set me alight
from the inside

- side effects

Alleycat

they all said
love is a two-way street
but when I looked around
you were nowhere to be seen
I anxiously paced the pavement
tapping my feet against the kerb
hoping to see you
drive down the avenue
it was at that moment I knew
I had been reading
the wrong signs
and the two-way street
where I thought we would meet
was just a dead-end alleyway
and the only person
standing there
was me
holding my broken heart

- wrong turn

how often
I find myself
sitting on the kitchen floor
falling apart
not wishing to get back up

- the lows

Alleycat

if time heals
can someone please tell me
where I can buy a time machine
so I can fast forward
to the part
where the memories
do not hurt anymore

- overwhelmed

breaking up with friends
is often more painful
than a partner
because it is
the kind of love
you do not expect to lose

- to lose a friend

Alleycat

I never knew
I could create
so many raindrops
from my eyes

- the flood

my issue
is not that
I am scared of love
but that
I am scared of losing it
because I have already lost it
too many times
and I am not sure
I will have the strength
to go on
if I were to lose it again

- scared to fall

Alleycat

I have tried
to move on
but each path I walk
leads me back to you

- struggling to walk away

at first
you stopped
saying goodnight
then you stopped
saying good morning
then you stopped
saying anything at all

- the beginning of the end

Alleycat

I know
I need to let this go
because we want different things
but just like magnets
when we get too close
we end up
all over each other

- attraction

I am sorry
I was not what you wanted
but I want you to know
I still want
to make you proud

- love letter

they say
part of healing
is admitting how you feel
but if I am being honest
I am not feeling
much at all

- numb

missing you
feels like I am living
within a world
separate from the one
I am already in
I can see and hear
everything around me
but I cannot connect
with any of it

- lost without you

Alleycat

I cannot say
I have been let down
because I am already
on the ground

- I am tired of your excuses

all I want to know is
if leaving me was worth it
otherwise all of the pain
I am feeling
was all for nothing

- when you left

Alleycat

how can I let you go
when you are
the best thing
I have ever found

- stay with me

Mark Donachie

what brought you to this city
he asks me
and all I can think
are all the things
that pushed me
so far from home

- a fresh start

Things that have helped me with the pain:

1. Going to therapy. Talking to a professional about what I was feeling and going through made the world seem a little less dark and helped me in many ways.

2. Energy healing. I never understood what it meant to be out of alignment, but when I started getting energy healing from a reiki healer near my hometown, it helped me become more grounded and feel less cloudy. It helped me so much that I trained in reiki myself and became a reiki master, which to this day, I am grateful for.

3. Finding presence. For so long, I lived inside my own head, forgetting that my body and the world around me existed. As hard as it is and continues to be, choosing to be present on this earth instead of escaping to my mind when things become overwhelming helps me. Think meditation, walks in nature, playing an instrument or listening to the world move around you. Those little moments of presence help me come back to myself.

4. Accepting people as they are. Do not tire yourself trying to convince others of your worth - you are already enough.

5. Allowing yourself to feel. It is ok to feel the deep seas of sadness when they appear, for we are all human, and emotions are part of our journey.

6. Do not be so hard on yourself. Often our biggest critics are ourselves. Be kind to yourself. You are doing your best, and that is all you can do.

7. Forcing myself to move my body. When I lived on the east coast, I found running along the beach helped me switch off for a while. To this day, exercising and lifting weights has helped me grow my confidence and always boosts my mood.

8. Choosing gratitude. Although not applicable to many situations, I think there is something to be said about finding gratitude in the little things, as it is often these little things that can bring us so much joy.

9. Connecting with spirit. I am no guru or spiritual master but connecting with spirit has helped me in many ways too. Learn to trust your path and ask for guidance when you need it.

10. Following your heart. Do not listen to what others tell you when it comes to love, life and your dreams. Even if things do not work out how you planned, it's better you tried than not at all. Be brave. Choose love, always.

Chapter Two
Love

Alleycat

every word
you say to me
gets written like pen to paper
inside of my head
so that on my darkest day
I can simply
pick up the pages
and read all of the reasons why
things are alright

- memories

even when I wilt
it will not matter
because you gave me so much life
that even sunlight was jealous of

- bouquet

there is nothing better
than when you look at me
between conversations
and I can feel
your want for me

- it's all in the eyes

who needs sleep
when everything
I could ever dream of
is standing in front of me
telling me
how much he adores me

- awake

if I had to choose someone
to be with forever
in this life
and every other
I would ask him to be mine
every single time

- forever and always

when I am around others
I often stay quiet
swallow my words as they stand
but with you
the words roll off my tongue
so effortlessly
almost involuntarily
as if each word
is desperate
to fall out in front of you
waiting to be recognised

- trust

Alleycat

his laugh
is the sound
my ears have been dreaming about
for their entire existence

- sweet melody

it fascinates me
how our hearts
will never see each other
yet still choose
to love one another
until the very end

- love is blind

self care is not optional
it is a must
if you want to help others
you must help yourself first

- you are a priority

even if others
catch my eye
I know for certain
they will never
catch my heart
the same way you did

- it will always be you

why does the space between us
feel like galaxies apart
I do not want to sit
across from you
I want to be
as close as humanly possible
to smell the cologne
directly from your neck
our faces mushed together
your arms like vines
around my back
addicted to your energy
I simply cannot get enough

- closer

the guards of my heart
all stepped aside
when you pulled me
into your arms
and held me so tight
all of the pain
started to fade
and I started to feel love again

- thank you

you are the sun
I am the moon
an endless cycle
of trying to reach one another
with no victory
so we watch each other
from afar
glowing in different ways
hoping that one day
we collide

- shine

if it is not him
it is no one else
I will happily wait
until the next life
just so we can try again
because he is the only one
that makes me feel this way

- one in a million

when I look at you
all I see is forever

- visions

the love I feel for you
is stronger than anything
I have ever known
and if I am fortunate enough
to get to be yours
I will consider myself
the luckiest man
on the planet

- to love you is a privilege

separation should not be feared

sometimes we must

walk our own paths

to understand ourselves

our own souls

on a deeper level

so that when

the universe decides

to bring us back together

we are not only

in a position

to be whole on our own

but that we are able

to be in harmony with another

- twin flame

you taught me how to say goodbye
to all of the ghosts that haunt me

- letting go

Alleycat

if another man
kissing me is wrong
then you definitely
do not want to know
all the ways
he loves me every night

- love in the dark

I love how we fall asleep
your body a frame
mine a picture
neatly sealed together
held tightly in place
until the sun wakes up
and tells us
it's time
to start the day

- picture perfect

the only good thing
about our goodbyes
is the kiss we share
that leaves me smiling
until I see you again

- kiss me goodbye

I was scared
I would never feel butterflies again
but I recently learned
they have been there all along
but they were just waiting
for the right person
to fly for

- butterflies

I never thought
I would give in
and let love win
but with you
I am now questioning
why I ever tried
to protect myself
because I now understand
there is nothing
to be afraid of

- safe in your love

love will appear
when it is meant to

- divine timing

Alleycat

I have made peace
with the fact
that if we ever end
I will spend
the rest of my life
getting over you

- a risk worth taking

unconditional love
is the ability
to love someone
so deeply
with no expectation
of an outcome

- true love

you look most beautiful
when you choose to be yourself

- unique

I will carry
our memories
in my heart forever
a museum of gratitude
for how you made me feel

- grateful

you were always enough
the same way
you are enough now
and always will be

- let go of expectations

the love I have for you
is so deep
it makes the ocean envious

- never ending

Alleycat

how silly you are
to think you do not matter
or that you cannot make
a difference to this world

- we cannot do this without you

all I ask
is for time not to fly
but to delay itself
because no matter
how many hours
we have together
it always goes too fast

- time flies

for me
to love myself
is a foreign land
I struggle to travel
but I still love myself enough
to keep trying
as I still believe
one day
it will all be worth it

- the journey

just like the waves
of the ocean
rush into the arms of the sand
you are the one
gravity pulls me home to
day after day
night after night

- you are my shoreline

self love is not always easy
some days
you need to force yourself
to do things
for your highest good
to keep yourself accountable
for everything
you want to accomplish

- momentum

Mark Donachie

I want to take care of you
in all the ways
no one ever has

- let me love you

Alleycat

please abandon the belief
that you need to be fully healed
in order to be loved
this is not true
sometimes our souls
evolve the best
when they heal
alongside another
that understands the pain
just as much as you

- when two become one

if it were possible
I would take
all of your pain
and carry it for you
just so you
could feel yourself again

- anything for you

Alleycat

your mouth is the sea
my tongue is a boat
with every voyage
we set sail
a different adventure

- every kiss is unique

to love
is to listen
to understand
to show patience
to hold space
to take care of

- to love is to be love

Alleycat

you say
that calling me
at the end of your day
is your favourite part
but my day does not begin
until I hear your voice

- you make me come alive

someday
you are going to be
the love of someone's life
you will be their highlight
their ever-lasting sunlight
loved deeper
than you have ever known
so do not give up
you may feel as though
you do not have
any love in this world
but one day
you will be the entire world
for someone else

- bright side

Alleycat

when they ask
how much do you love him
I will say
enough to risk everything for
and more than enough
to shout his name
from the rooftops

- to choose love

I am not jealous
of your previous lovers
in fact
I would like to thank them
for letting you go
so I could find you

- the past led us here

do not feel guilty
for choosing your own happiness
yes we must
often factor others in
in certain circumstances
but overall
you need to do
what makes you happy
and what you love
because we do not get
that much time to spend
with mother earth
so do not
waste it doing things
you feel no love for

- follow your heart

love yourself enough
to let go
of anyone
and anything
that is not meant for you

- now is the time

how can you think
you are not loved
have you not seen
the way the sun
kisses your skin
how it leaves your body red
because it adores you so much
or how the rain
lavishly bathes in your skin
at every opportunity it gets
have you not heard
the trees
whisper their excitement
to one another
as you walk under their shoulders
or how the birds
sing you melodies
while you get ready for the day
so if you think
you are not loved
I ask you
to think again

- love is all around us

one of my earliest memories of love
is my father
carrying me over his shoulder
through the broken hospital doors
because the pain in my chest
would not let me breathe

- hero

you must take
every chance you get
when it comes to love
because it does not
come around often

- allow yourself to be vulnerable

how strange it is
that when he wears
nothing but black
he still shines brighter
than everyone else
in the room

- a keeper

Alleycat

I know
I say it all the time
but I am so grateful
to be with you

- never forget how much I love you

we kissed so much
your chin went red

- passion

Alleycat

I still remember
the bar in the city centre
where we met
one night after class
I sat in my chair
with swimming pools
in my palms
my heart exhausted
from running laps
around my chest
as you looked at the menu
I thought about my words
and how the more I waited
the less chance of arrival
so I said with such speed
that I do not walk a straight line
that I walk a rainbow line instead
to which you said
that is nice
what do you want to drink
and I simply smiled
and remembered
this is why we are friends

- eighteen

you walked
straight out of my dreams
into my reality
and I have been sleepwalking
ever since

- I must be dreaming

Alleycat

if they do not love you
for being yourself
then you must leave
because you cannot
live in a home
that you have outgrown
you must find
a new place to thrive
to come alive
because what you will find
is that there is
no better place to be
than to be yourself
surrounded by others
or to be happy
in your own company
after many years
of only being happy
for someone else's

- time to leave

you do not understand
I cannot fall for you
because if I did
I would not be able
to get back up

- falling in love

Alleycat

do you remember
the four leaf clover
you gave me
one night after dinner
you said
put out your hand
and in it placed a piece
of green string
than ran through a hole
in a silver clover
that same night
I put it in my wallet
and it has not moved since
because each day
it reminds me
of how lucky I am
to have ever met you

- lucky charm

the mountains
on his back
I could trek
with my fingers
for hours on end

- mountaineer

Alleycat

if you are looking
for the love of your life
stand in front of the mirror
and tell yourself
I am all the love I need
and from there
the rest will fall into place

- it all starts with you

if I could choose
what my last moment could be
I would choose
your eyes
looking into mine
as I slowly fall asleep
to wake up waiting
on the other side
for you to join me
when the time is divine

- the finale

Chapter Three

Finding Strength

to feel pain
does not mean
you are weak
it means
you are strong enough
to be vulnerable

- allow yourself to feel

because when it comes to love
you're supposed to follow your heart
so if it breaks
know that it is ok
because at some moment in time
it was worth breaking for
and that is why
you followed it in the first place

- give yourself a break

Alleycat

you only want me
when you're drunk
but the funny part is
I do not want you at all

- stay gone

I am
starting to make waves
but one day
I will create storms

- my strength is growing

Alleycat

there is a line
of who I was before
and who I was
once I crossed it
and I am never going back

- making progress

when you take him
back to your apartment
and sit on the couch
with the blanket that I bought you
from that Sunday market
while you weren't looking
I can guarantee
it will keep you warmer
than he ever will

- irreplaceable

Alleycat

at first
I blamed the distance
then I blamed myself
for not being enough to conquer it
but the actual blame
belonged to you

- self worth

I would rather
be hated for being myself
than be loved
for being someone else

- inner strength

save your heart
for someone that deserves it

- do not settle

you told me
that you lead me on
because you weren't sure
what you wanted
but I am not a supermarket
I am not a convenience store
you cannot walk
between the aisles of me
pick up your favourite things
and leave
when your basket is full

- 24/7

Alleycat

you said
you wanted someone better
but better
slipped right through your fingers

- hindsight

you are not
the voices in your head
or the monsters under your bed
you are the space in between
you are the observer
good and bad
just observe

- meditation

Alleycat

do not let
anyone convince you
that being kind is a weakness
for your kindness
is a rare gift
that many people
will never understand
or ever receive

- be kind

you stole my light
but you forgot
I am made from lightning

- this one is for you

Alleycat

the fact
you are still here
even when the pain convinced you
that it was not worth staying
only proves
how strong you are

- you are not your pain

your strength
is a structure
the more you build it
the more resilient
it becomes

- one day at a time

let go of all the anger
at this point
the only blood you are boiling
is your own

- breathe

my name
has always been written in the stars
but you were too busy
being blinded by your own
to notice mine

- your ego will be your downfall

Alleycat

I am too soft for revenge
but I am strong enough to know
that karma always wins
and I am sure
that one day
your empire will shatter
and I will watch
from the sidelines
observing in silence
not because I want you to suffer
but because maybe only then
will you learn
that hurting others
in order for you to succeed
only results
in you hurting yourself

- what goes around comes around

Mark Donachie

to me
death is not a grim reaper
but a party planner
because when it is my turn
to be surprised
with a celebration
I did not expect
I will enter with excitement
because I will be
surrounded by all of the people
I lost over the years
and we will dance together
all night long
making up for the time we lost
that we can now get lost in
every night
for the rest of time

- this party is to die for

Alleycat

you have spent
far too long
hiding your talents
that the world is looking for
you already know
what to do
just let it flow
because your gifts
have a power
that can help
change this world
for the better

- what are you waiting for

I was
a constellation of candles
sparkling on a birthday cake
forever changing
just to give you more chances
but each time I did
you blew them all

- my wish is for you to leave

so long
as the sun exists
there will always be
light in this world

- hope

trust that
what you are looking for
will find you
when it is meant to

- destiny

Alleycat

I used to think
everything I did
was never good enough
but I was mistaken
for I have always been enough
just not for you

- reflecting

pain
is the toughest teacher
but through it
you will learn the most

- understanding

Alleycat

no longer
will I work myself to death
or try so hard
to prove that I am enough

- I am already a success

people like you
are all the same
craving the attention
but once you get the hit
you vanish like the smoke
from your mouth

- exhale

sometimes
no matter how hard you try
it does not work
but that does not mean
that you failed
all it means is that
it was not destined to be
and that you are meant
for something greater

- trust your path

I was enough
before you met me
and I will still be enough
if you ever leave

- secure

you think you are not strong
yet you are still here
and that in itself
is worth celebrating

- little victories

when I walk into a room
I fill it with my own light
because I have learned
I can shine
just as bright
without you

- growth

Alleycat

if I am going to stay
I am going to give this life
everything I have
and cherish every moment

- trying my best

you have been conditioned to believe
that the most authentic version of yourself
is not what the world wants
but please remember
the most unique parts of yourself
are what make you special

- be yourself

Alleycat

it is funny
how quick you are
to take the credit
when you did nothing
to help me get it

- this was all me

I should have known
to leave you
when you accidentally sent me
a photo of your old lover
but I gave you
the benefit of the doubt
or when you cancelled
our dinner with friends
after I was already dressed
and ready to go
because you got cold feet
if I could go back in time
I would give my head a shake
and tell myself
just because he is a mature age
does not mean
he is a mature man

- I deserved better

maybe
I was not raised wrong
perhaps there was no stopping
my ability to shine

- proud

when you feel lonely
always remember
that everything is connected

- we are all one

strength is not just physical
it is emotional
but also mental and spiritual
all four combined
are what make you strong
and by allowing these
to work in harmony
you can learn
to create balance
within yourself

- finding strength

I wish
you never had to leave
although it gives me comfort
knowing that I am still able
to connect with you

- the bridge between worlds

Alleycat

I have never met someone
with so much strength
to show up each day
and give it your all
despite all the sadness
you have had
to go through

- one of the many reasons why I love you

take a moment
to congratulate yourself
on how far
you have come

- you are a champion

only in our darkest moments
are we so open to the light

- turning point

it is ok
to wish someone farewell
but still miss them
as they slowly move on

- let go of what is not meant for you

I will
continue to hope
because that is all
I have left

- keeping positive

things have not been
the easiest for you
and each day may feel
like a battle to get through
but do not forget
you are a warrior
you have conquered
every other day
why let today be different
summon your strength
take a breath
and keep going

- you are so powerful

Alleycat

by the time
you change your mind
for the tenth time
I will already be gone
and your name on my phone
will be nothing more
than eleven numbers
I do not recognise

- moving on

my body
is not the strongest
my mind
is not the wisest
but the magic
that runs through my veins
is limitless
and that
is all that matters

- bloodline

Alleycat

I find no pleasure
in payback
only spirit knows
how much you deserve it
but sour sticks
and I prefer to be sweet
although I cannot say the same
for all the others
you have crossed

- your future is looking sour

you would think
a break up would hurt me
but the truth is
I have been met
by far worse things
than a lover
who no longer wants me

- this will not break me

perhaps
we are all just stars
trying to shine
as best as we can

- galaxy

if you cannot find the light
then you must become it

- go inward

Alleycat

I will not let you
turn my dreams into darkness
just because
you do not believe

- watch me shine

I used
to walk past your house
on my way
to meet friends in the city
forever nervous
in case we met
or if I saw you
with someone new
but now all I can think is
I hope you see me
so you can see
that I am doing fine
without you

- moving forward

Alleycat

when I start to feel sad
about what we could have been
I remind myself
that the universe
always has a plan
and mine is yet to unfold

- better things are coming

I have learned
to always say
how I feel
because I do not want
to spend my life
surrounded by envelopes
with all the messages
I refused to deliver
from my heart
to my tongue

- love letters

Alleycat

my phone still tells me
the last time
you were on yours
but at least I know
that you are doing ok
and I only hope
whoever you are talking to
treats you
with all the love you deserve

- speak soon

the ones
that have broken my heart the most
are also the ones
that have taught me
how much strength I have

- inner power

after all this time
it does still hurt
and that is more than ok

- waves of emotion

as I sit
on the hill
that overlooks the city
I now call home
my mind starts to think
how far I have come

from the pain
of choosing myself
to the heartbreaks
of loving another
I still remember
the first night
falling apart
under different stars
to years later
dancing among them

it is only now
that I realise
I may be alone
but I am surrounded
by everything I need

- alleycat